Don't Post That!

Your Guide to Keeping a Good Online Reputation

John W. Bowlin, Sr.

ISBN-13: 978-1500585266

DEDICATION

To Katie ... for loving and supporting me. To say my life has been greatly enriched by having you in my life would be an understatement.

To Mary ... for your undying support, and giving of your time unselfishly. Sometimes a simple thank you doesn't seem to be adequate enough.

To Kim ... for your friendship and encouragement. It's wonderful having a friend like you in my life.

... and to the many others who have continually offered me support and encouragement, I want to thank you for following me as I fulfill my dreams. You all have a special place in my heart and in my life.

Table of Contents

4

Introduction:

Today's technology is fantastic. You can keep in touch with people all across the world quickly and easily through options such as email and social networking. The words that you post on your blog right now are readable by someone thousands of miles away as soon as you publish.

What a Wonderful Time

It's a wonderful time to be alive with all of the tech devices we have today that border on science fiction.

If you were to just step into the world today, you might think that these devices meant to bring us all closer together would have been able to create a veritable utopia.

Of course, we know that is not at all what the Internet is today. As much as it offers, and though it has nearly unlimited potential, for many, it really becomes a place to look at pictures of cats and to criticize, ostracize, and demoralize other people and businesses for any little thing possible. It also becomes a place of regrets, as in, "Oh, man, I probably shouldn't have posted that."

What Is Wrong With These People?

That same person who stepped into today's world and wondered at the power of the Internet will also wonder just what is wrong with the people using it. Some of them are trolls who want nothing more than to derail every conversation and to hurt every person imaginable.

Others are posting updates and photos that they probably shouldn't. They are sending text messages laced with dynamite and C4 to friends, coworkers, and strangers without ever realizing that it could come back to haunt them.

People love the Internet, but they really do seem to be rather stupid about how they are using it! Not all people are like this, and you do not have to be one that is.

Not Like the Others

Use your head, think about what you are doing online, and think about how your photos, videos, and posts will affect others, and in turn, how that will ultimately affect you. Use your head and your common sense, and if something seems like it *might* be a bad idea, here's a news flash; it's a bad idea. So, *don't post that!*

This book delves into the darker corners of the Internet to show you where some of the dangers are and what you will need to do if you hope to avoid those issues. We discuss how posting without thinking can damage your personal life, your work life, and your own brand.

Let's get started.

Chapter 1: Today's Shoot First, Apologize Later World

You hear about it all of the time. Someone on the web posted a compromising photo or said something impulsively and rashly without thinking about the consequences it could have. Maybe you've even done this a time or two in the past and now you are looking for ways to rectify your behavior.

Why Is Impulsive Posting Such a Problem Today?

What is it about today that has made the world seemingly go mad and start posting and writing without care or concern over what consequences their actions bring? A couple of different things are likely at play here.

No One Will See It

First, people don't always realize the reach that their posts have. When they put something up online for others to see, it can take on a life of its own very quickly. Something that you post and feel is semi-private amongst friends or family can quickly turn viral. If you post something that you shouldn't have, the tide will turn against you sooner than you might think, and even those family and friends might start to distance themselves from you a bit.

They'll Never Know

Second, many people have some sort of feeling of disconnect when they are posting online. Since it is not a face-to-face interaction with someone, it provides a bit of distance. When people post on blogs for forums, or on comments for articles, they tend to have a sense of anonymity, which makes them say things that they might not normally say. The truth is, in today's world, there really is very little anonymity, and the things that you say, post and do can come back to bite you. We'll look at some real world examples of that in a later chapter in this book.

What Do You Mean It's Not Funny?

Third, humor can be very subjective. A joke or photo that one person might feel is funny and entirely appropriate can strike another person as banal or downright offensive.

In the 1990s, there was a famous case where a man got in trouble for retelling a joke from *Seinfeld* at work. One of his coworkers found it offensive and sued for sexual harassment. When this happened, it was big news for quite some time. People actually followed the court case.

Today, because of the ease with which the Internet allows us to communicate, this sort of thing – offending someone and getting in trouble for it – happens on a nearly daily basis.

Who Cares?

Some people out there say and do things without really caring what their words or actions do to others, and this is the fourth reason some people post without thinking.

While they might not be out and out sociopaths, there are many who simply do not care that others may find their opinions or photos offensive. These types of people do what they want to do, offend who they want, and always seem to wonder just why they have so few people in their life who actually want to be around them!

Hard to Judge

Fifthly, the world and the people in it can be hard to judge. While jokes from *Seinfeld* might have been reason enough for someone to sue in the past, times have seriously changed. Today's media is far different, and tends to have graphic sexual and violent content, more so than in the past.

For many, it really can be difficult to know what you should or should not post, say and do while on the Internet because of this. It can be almost impossible to understand how people will react. This often leads to people saying and writing things without really thinking about what they are doing. Will talking about the last episode of *Game of Thrones* get them in trouble if they talk about some of the sexual content?

It can be hard to gauge the temperature of a group of people when it comes to what they will and will not find offensive. It's even easy to offend friends and family you think you know well, so it's that much easier to offend people you barely know, or don't know, on the web.

Be Like Spock

For those unfamiliar, Spock, a character on *Star Trek*, is a Vulcan. He does not exhibit emotion and always thinks logically and rationally before acting. People who have the ability to roam freely about the Internet should really take a lesson from Mr. Spock and start to use logical and rational thought before they begin typing their missives and posting racy photos best kept private.

However, we aren't aliens. We're human, and that means we are very flawed in this regard. When we are excited about something, we tend to want to share it with the world. The same is true when we are angry or outraged. The Internet has given everyone the ability to voice his or her opinion, no matter what it is. People really take advantage of this for good and ill.

When they see something on the web that angers them, whether it is an article or blog post, a post on a social network, or even an email they get, they fire off

15

responses in the heat of the moment. This is the *worst* time to do this because it means they aren't thinking clearly. Impulsiveness and loss of emotion are *easily* among of the top reasons the Internet seems full of vitriol, hate, and spite all the time! We've even devoted the entire next chapter to it.

Take a Breath or Two

Ultimately, if you feel as though you have to ask yourself whether or not what you are posting could be offensive or if it could anger someone else, the short answer is simply don't post it. Wait a bit, take a breath or two and think about how others might react to what you are writing, and then decide if it *really* is necessary. If the only reason you are posting is to get a reaction out of someone, then chances are you should *not* post it at all.

Finally, remember that just because you have something to say and the right to say it doesn't mean that everyone wants to hear it.

Chapter 2: Emotion and Impulse – The Bane of the Internet

How are you when it comes to controlling your emotions? While you might think you are calm, cool, and collected under pressure, it's time that you were honest with yourself. What grinds your gears and gets under your skin? What irks you to no end? What makes you angry and gets you emotional?

Chances are that you are like most people, and you will find quite a few different things that rile you up online and that might make you want to lash out and type something without really thinking about the outcome.

Let's look at a few of the commonalities that make people upset on the web so you can see what gets at you the most. Maybe it is one of these elements. Maybe it is something else entirely.

Stupid Opinions Are Valid Opinions

The Internet is a perfect place for discourse for many topics. However, you have to realize that many people out there will not hold the same opinions as you hold. Some people will have opinions that you find downright stupid, and they will shout them as loudly as possible on the web. While you might not respect their opinion, and you might think it is a stupid or ignorant way of thinking, spouting off at them will *not* change their mind on any subject.

It will simply evolve into the both of you saying things that you will regret at some point because irrational emotion and anger take over your brain and leak down to your fingers until you are typing nonsense.

People will have their opinions and you will have your opinions. Some people out there feel that Michael Bay's Transformers series is the best thing to happen to cinema since the invention of the movie camera. Others know better, but both opinions are valid simply because they are opinions.

It is important to separate facts and opinions when you are reading information on the web. It's equally as important to realize that you shouldn't attack someone's opinions because it will simply lead to fights.

Politics and Religion

They say there are two things you should never talk about in polite company, namely politics and religion. Keep in mind that the people of the Internet are certainly not polite company, but you should still keep your views and opinions on these things to a minimum unless you want to start arguments online.

Take a moment to head online and look up an article on... nearly anything. Read the comments and see how long it takes before the discussion devolves into some diatribe about religion or politics. It happens all of the time, and it happens faster than you might think.

Biased Articles

The legion of people commenting on the Internet is certainly not the only thing that will get an emotional response from you. Sometimes, the actual articles, posts, and videos will get your blood boiling and make you want to leave a comment voicing your anger.

Just as you need to exercise caution when interacting with other people commenting on the web, you have to do the same when it comes to leaving comments on the article. It could start a fight with the person who posted the piece, or with others commenting. Think about the words you use as well as how you post first.

Never post angry. Create thought out responses that make sense and that you can back up with facts.

Never attack and never retaliate. Be above those actions, and you will find that you have far less trouble with your web interactions.

Oh, the Trolls Are Thick in This Part of the Internet Forest

Trolls aren't just monsters under bridges. No, they have taken to populating the Internet, filling it with their brand of stupidity, and they will often try to bait people, good people such as you, into wars on the web. In those wars, you will inevitably start to say things or make claims without thinking them through entirely. If you aren't careful, you could be the one who ends up looking like the fool at the end of the day.

It is important to remember that, as pleasant as the web and all of those other technologies can be, they have their downsides as well, their dark side, if you will. A large population on the Internet is full of spite and anger, and they can easily draw you into their shenanigans if you aren't careful! It is important that you "Just Say No" Nancy Reagan style when you are dealing with these trolls.

Of course, this is often easier to say than it is to do. Trolls are magical and malicious creatures that seem to have the capability of baiting even the best of us into imaginary wars of great proportions as we vie for Internet dominance… whatever that is.

How to Avoid the Trolls and Their Troll Traps

Learn to spot the trolls in order to avoid their traps. These people are desperately seeking some type of attention online. They are looking to make you angry and frustrated, and they generally follow certain patterns. They may not always be easy to identify, but it is possible to do with a few simple tips.

When you come across a comment, read between the lines. What is the purpose of the comment? Does it appear as though it is trying to provoke a reaction? Then chances are good it is a troll. If they say something that is defamatory or that talks about nonsense or makes a blatantly stupid or obtuse statement, chances are it is a troll trap.

If the comment makes you feel angry or upset in the slightest, chances are they are a troll, or they are simply an angry and hateful person. Either way, you do not want to interact with the person. Simply avoid the comment.

You can also check their profile and their comment history through most sites. Check to see what other types of things they've posted. If he or she is trolling, or are just angry at the world, you will see this in their previous posts. This will tell you quite a bit about the person, and will let you know you should avoid him or her at all costs. If they are an anonymous user, a masked troll, then you can be sure they are not on the up and up too.

There is a saying that's quite popular when it comes to these folks. Don't feed the trolls. This simply means that you should ignore them and pretend they don't exist. They want attention and when you give it, they will keep on with their actions. Ignoring them makes them go away most of the time.

If you find that the troll won't go away or starts to harass you, it's time to contact an administrator for the site. This is far better than engaging the person. The administrator will hopefully take care of it for you. If the admin does nothing, then it might be time to rethink your use of that particular site.

Troll Tracks

Here's a quick and handy list of things to look for when you think you might be dealing with trolls. Refer to it often, and you will soon see patterns in their behavior, making the vile little things easier to avoid.

- Bad grammar
- Typing in all caps
- Lack of real knowledge
- Bad science
- Holier than thou attitude
- Bad understanding of the legal system and Constitution
- Pretending to be an expert
- Only *their* opinion matters

- Intolerant of others beliefs, views, race, sex, sexual orientation, or anything else

What Really Motivates the Trolls?

Trolls and other Internet baddies are looking to get a rise out of you. They are looking for attention and confrontation.

Of course, they don't generally want to have a real confrontation. They are the worst kind of cowards – the type who will hide behind their computer screen, safe in their little troll den, as they continue to try to bait you into a war that could damage your reputation, and certainly your happiness, while they go along contentedly looking for another victim.

Because they have that anonymity, or near anonymity that the Internet provides, they become essentially invisible and feel that they are safe from danger. This empowers them to say whatever nastiness comes to mind without fear of repercussion. Many begin to shut off their empathy and pretend that the people they are tormenting online aren't real people at all.

Psychologically speaking, this is akin to sociopathic behavior, albeit the "lite" version of a sociopath. They don't have any visual cues from the other person to see how they are affecting them, so they do not behave the way they might normally act in an actual face-to-face encounter. Everything is words on a screen, and it can be quite easy to fall into this trap of not understanding the *feelings* those words cause the person on the other end of the connection.

You don't want this to happen to you, so whenever you are writing anything online, always remember that other people out there, real people with feelings and everything, are going to read it or see it. Think before you post and think before you reply. The only thing replying to a troll will do is bring even more negativity into the world.

It can be extremely difficult to discover the *real* motivations behind trolling though, because the trolls themselves rarely know the reason, and they don't acknowledge it if they do. Trolls are secretive, and they don't want others to know what they do, especially other people in their real life. Imagine how you would look at a family member if you discovered he was spending time each day trolling forums and being a complete pain. It's childish behavior – and sometimes it is kids, generally male teens, who are doing it. However, adults can be just as guilty.

The most common reasons that people troll tend to fall into a select number of categories. Sometimes, the reason can be a blend of several of these potential motives.

Let's look at some of those motives.

- Boredom
- Fun/humor
- Need for attention
- Pure cruelty
- Sense of disenfranchisement and frustration that makes them lash out in a secretive, but no less destructive, manner

Who Are the Trolls?

The popular image of an Internet troll is a young male in his teens or twenties who is angry, intolerant, and who wants desperately for people he will never meet to give him attention. While this might be the typical troll, he is not the only species of troll out there. No, there are quite a few subspecies out there as well.

Some of the most common types of trolls you will run across on the Internet include the following:

- **The Hateful Troll** – He or she hates everything and has something negative to say about it no matter what it is.

- **The Yelling Troll** – This troll is very angry about *stuff* and wants everyone to know it, thus the abuse of the caps lock key.

- **The Grammar/Knowledge Troll** – Good grammar and accurate information is important, but these folks take it to an entirely new level, pointing out every little inaccuracy to the point of pure annoyance. Anyone familiar with the old cartoon *The Smurfs* will recognize that Brainy Smurf would fall into the category of a grammar/knowledge troll.

- **The Out of Context Troll** – This troll will take everything you say out of context and will try to turn it against you, trying to make you sound like an idiot, a jerk, a misogynist, and other dastardly things every chance they get.

- **Evangelist Troll** – No matter what subject, whether you are talking about your favorite television show, a game, or the state of NASA, these trolls will turn the comment section into a theological debate.

- **The Political "Genius" Troll** – The political genius troll feels that he or she knows everything about politics and the Constitution, although they usually just spout off things they heard on television. There is no reasoning with these trolls and they come from all parts of the political spectrum. They are vicious, and like the preaching trolls, will argue to the death.

- **The Dull Knife Troll** – The harsh truth of the world is that some people are simply not intelligent... at all. Yet, the Internet gives them a platform to talk. These trolls honestly might not even know they are trolling. It is still a good practice to avoid them though.

- **Spoiler Troll** – You know your favorite TV show? These trolls know it, too, and they will gleefully post spoilers without giving any warning.

- **Gruff and Humorless Troll** – These trolls have no sense of humor, or they miss jokes entirely and suddenly feel offended by not knowing something. They will then start sending angry messages and replies.

- **Attention Troll** – These trolls are a bit different, because they are not always mean or spiteful. However, they can turn in an instant. Here's how they work. They like to go fishing. They will post a comment or a post on a social network site that has some bait on it, such as "I can't believe that just happened to me". When you respond, you are taking that hook, and then they reel you in, telling you something along the lines of "it doesn't matter" or "it's none of your business." They actually get angry towards you. Some do this regularly as a means of getting attention and then rebuking friends and strangers who comment. Trolls are funny this way.

So, there is no single, perfectly identifiable profile for a troll. Nearly anyone can say and do things online that will get them into trouble, and nearly anyone can turn into a troll at some point. Even you if you are not careful.

The Internet Can Be a Sad Place

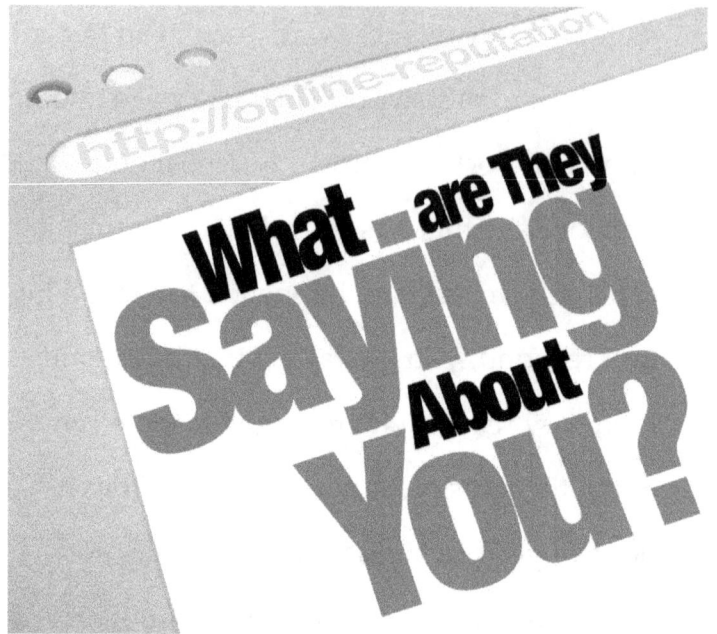

Take a moment to head to a couple of different sites online. Go to YouTube and check out a couple of videos, popular and otherwise, and then read the comments. You will undoubtedly see comments that range from helpful, fun and supportive to those simply full of anger and hate directed at the creator for no reason other than the fact that the trolls and rotten people of the world want to find an outlet to abuse others.

Do the same thing on some of the other sites that you read regularly, and sites that you've never read before. See how long it takes before someone insults another person in the comments section. It usually happens on the first page.

This is highly unfortunate, but the web works this way today because people can hide behind a shell of anonymity. Hiding in this manner, even if they are on camera and making angry videos, separates them from the real world. They feel they can get away with far more because it is "just the Internet".

What Do You Do?

If you have a blog, a YouTube channel, a social networking account, or you post *anything* online, you will have to deal with these types of people sometimes. It's an unfortunate fact of the Internet. Your immediate reaction is to defend yourself or to defend the person who created the content. Before long, you are arguing with someone you will probably never meet in real life.

They will hurl insults, and so will you. How long will it be before you say something truly regrettable? When you are angry, you may type things you would never really say in real life. This is where the danger lies when it comes to your reputation online, and offline for that matter.

Grow a thick skin and try not to let the comments bother you. Is this an easy thing to do? No, it's not, at least for most people. Some people may have more trouble letting these things go than others will. If they get to you too much, *stop reading them.*

Simply stop.

You might even want to take a bit of a break from the Internet when you do this. Clear your mind and remind yourself that the vast majority of the people on the web simply don't matter in your life. They aren't your family and your friends, they don't really know you, and they have plenty of their own issues. They are nothing more than digital phantoms.

It's Not ALL Bad

Even though there are quite a few people out there on the web that can derail your train of thought and that can make your rage and anger build up to Hulk-like levels in a matter of minutes when you see or listen to their drivel, it's not all bad.

In fact, there are some great people and places to visit on the Internet. Find them, enjoy and love them, and make sure you are on your best behavior.

Don't let the bad eggs out there turn *you* into an Internet monster. Don't let them make you post things that you shouldn't simply because you want to find a way to retaliate or to humiliate them.

Those are all childish games, and you need to stay as far away from them as possible if you hope to make it out of this Internet alive and with your dignity intact. After all, you don't want to become the thing that angered you in the first place… you don't want to become a jerk or a troll.

As upset as you might be, and as much as you might want to say something to hurt someone who hurt you, you are *not* that type of person. You are better than that, so don't let the Internet populace think you are just another member of the lowbrow crowd out there.

More than Impulse Retaliation Causes Internet Problems

Of course, impulse posting when you are angry is just one of the many ways that you can get into trouble with the things you say and do on the web. Emotion is generally at the crux of it though, and it can cause some serious issues, which we will look at throughout the rest of this book.

Chapter 3: How to Get in Trouble on the Internet… and How to Avoid It

In the last chapter, we talked quite a bit about the amount of anger and frustration that the web can brew inside of you, often due to the amount of trolling and general nonsense that happens on the

Internet. It was important to learn about trolling behavior so that you can do two things.

1. Avoid the trolls, as interacting with them is one of the *fastest and surest* ways of saying things you regret on the Internet.
2. Avoid actually becoming a troll and getting into trouble.

Of course, we also mentioned that the Internet has a number of different ways that you can get into some hot water if you aren't careful. It's time to look a little more closely at some of those things now.

Sharing Is...

You know the term "sharing is caring", but in today's Internet age, we should really be thinking about adopting another term instead. How about, "over sharing is blatantly stupid" or something along those lines that might be a bit less offensive.

While this might sound a bit harsh, think about how many times you've seen things online that are simply too much. Your friends and family, and even you, are probably guilty of this at some point. How many times have you seen someone spout off about something that came back to haunt them? If you look close enough, you can see this happening every day on most social networks and other places on the web, as well.

People share *everything* online today, and it might be a very good idea if they didn't, for them and for the rest of the world. There is such a thing as putting out too much information.

Most of the time, it is little innocuous things that will not matter to the grand scheme of your world. However, there are always those out there that decide to go a little further than they should.

Think before you post.

Always.

If there is ever even a sliver of doubt in your mind then *don't post that!*

The Times, They Are a-Changing

The Internet is a very weird place today. Think about it for a moment. Those who are of a certain age – those who are at least in their mid-20s and older, likely remember a time before the Internet was as widespread as it is today. Yes, youngsters, there was a time *before* the Internet.

Back in Time

Imagine for a moment that it is 1985 again. If you weren't around then, pretend you step into a time machine and are trying to blend into the times. Now, let's say you are having a meal at home. Perhaps you cooked a nice steak or some fish or whatever and it really turns your taste buds on. Would you whip out a camera, take a picture, and then show it to everyone that you meet? Would you call up your friends and tell them what you are eating? Would you tell people random and mundane things throughout the day? Well, that last part has always been a part of some peoples' live!

What changed? The advent of the Internet and advanced technology for our phones and computers, naturally. They present something of a paradox. We are more easily able to connect with people all around the world. However, the things we do with technology tend to pull us out of the real world and pull us away from actual social interactions. People text more than talk; they post to one another on Facebook more than they actually visit one another.

Look at most of the posts on Twitter and Facebook today, and you'll find deep and thought provoking missives such as, "waited at the dentist's office for two hours, smh", or "going to Burger King for lunch". We are taking things that no one in their right mind really cares about other than the person posting them and making them mini headlines in the story that is our lives. It might be better to save the posts for things that really matter!

Post, but Be Careful!

Of course, there is nothing inherently wrong with sharing this kind of innocent information. It's mundane and generally boring to most people who do not know you, but this type of posting can't get you into any trouble at home or at work, or with the rest of the Internet, at least most of the time.

Once again, you always have to think before posting and try to put yourself in the shoes of other people who might see it. What would some of those trolls from the last chapter do if they saw the post?

Throughout this chapter, we'll look at some of the many different ways that people are able to get themselves into some sort of trouble, large and small, on the Internet today. By learning how people get into trouble, it should help you learn the best ways to avoid that trouble.

What People Hate

If you want to have some quick and surefire tips not to raise the ire of people on the Internet, then this is the section for you. By adhering to the information here, it can help to keep you out of the way of Internet anger and wrath.

Let's look at the things that people absolutely despise on the web, and often in real life too, so you can learn *not to do them*.

Sarcasm

Sarcasm can be extremely funny at times. Entire careers have stemmed from using sarcasm as a form of comedy. However, you have to remember that when you are typing words online, it's extremely difficult to show that you are being sarcastic and not serious. It becomes very easy to come off like a real jerk when you try to use sarcasm on the web.

Some people just don't get sarcasm, which gives it the potential to be even more inflammatory without even trying. If you have a great sarcastic comment that you really want to post online… just don't do it. While some people might think it is funny and get it, others will not. They will be upset, and the funny little thing that you post could end up causing a world of trouble for you. Getting a little laugh out of it simply is not worth the trouble it could cost.

In fact, many types of humor can be difficult to convey in writing and by people online who might not have the same sense of humor that you have. This leads to a number of problems for individuals and companies alike, as we will see in a later chapter.

Being General

This has nothing to do with the military. Instead, it has everything to do with not being specific! This is where many people get into some light trouble on the web... not really trouble so much as raising the ire of other posters and forum goers, which can eventually lead into an Internet battle.

Whenever you use a generalization, such as every man leaves up the toilet seat, or every teenager is addicted to their smartphones, people will come out of the woodwork to correct you. Generalizations in, well, general, are bad because they are never accurate.

However, most people use them to make a point, not to be accurate. Of course, people on the Internet, even though they might know this, will attack those generalizations. Just make sure that you know this and make sure that you avoid being general whenever you can.

Speaking as an Expert... Without Being an Expert

Did you know just how many experts there are on everything in this world? A few minutes on the Internet, and you'll see that everyone is an expert, at least according to them. Unless you are an *actual expert*, you should not try to act like one or talk like one.

It will only lead to someone with more knowledge putting you in your place before long. This doesn't mean you can't quote facts and write about facts, or even your opinion online. The web is all about that! However, you don't want to try to come off as knowing more about a subject than you really do.

Needing to do more and more research and to keep those oh-so-accurate Wikipedia pages open when you are trying to argue a point where you are an expert can be exhausting. It is better for you if you just don't do it.

Exaggeration

This falls into a similar category as sarcasm, meaning that many people simply don't get it. You might say something about the wait for the new season of *The Walking Dead* being a million years long and there will be some people out there who will come at you for this. They might tell you that it's actually only X amount of months, Y amount of days, and Z amount of hours... see how they aren't being general! Others might tell you to get a life and to get outside.

Both of these things can result in arguments that are about as sensible as the schoolyard fights over whose favorite superhero would win in a fight. Although, to be honest, superhero fights are actually a very big part of Internet fights for many adults today.

Yes, this is an *exaggerated* example, but the point is that people can get touchy about little exaggerations and big ones alike. Even though most people know the poster isn't serious about the exaggeration, it can still upset people.

Use exaggerations if you want – they aren't too big of a deal – but be ready for at least one or two people to respond negatively to it. Remember, this is the Internet. It's where people go to be negative.

Advice for Relationships

You've been in relationships before, both good and bad. Therefore, you are knowledgeable about every aspect of every relationship problem that could possibly affect a couple. Of course, you know that isn't true. You know that every relationship is different. So, make sure you don't give any relationship advice online, and never take sides in an argument. This is true online and offline.

Always avoid giving relationship advice, even if someone asks for it. When you post something online, everyone will see it. If the couple works things out, then you will be the jerk for writing what you did. When you write anything, others will come at you and accuse you of fanning the flames, or they will attack you for daring to give your opinion.

Even though you might have an opinion, and it might be valid, you really do want to keep it to yourself.

The Other Touchiest Subjects

Some things are perfect for brewing up anger online. You want to avoid posting on topics such as religion, politics, people's children, disciplinary methods for children, and similar subjects. Don't post about them and don't comment on other posts that are about them.

If you do start talking about these things, be ready for the problems and the angry Internet people that will eventually come your way. If you are an individual, then you might not mind so much. If you are running a business and trying to build a brand though, you will find that it can be quite damaging to you.

As always, use some sense when you are posting anywhere online, whether it is a social network, your site, your blog, or a forum. People can always find out who you are no matter how anonymous you think you might be.

How Have People Been in Legal Trouble Online?

Worrying about reputation and avoiding troll wars is just a part of the trouble that some people find online. Many people out there actually get into real legal trouble because they don't stop for a moment to use some common sense before they do something truly stupid on the web.

You are no dummy, and the chances of legal troubles such as the ones that follow happening to you are slim to none, but you still need to exercise caution and good judgment.

Let's look at what some real winners – that's sarcasm right there – have done to get in trouble on the web before. Don't worry; we'll go even deeper into what people have done to ruin themselves online in Chapter 8 with some real world examples.

Planning and Committing Crimes

Some people out there have actually used the Internet, including social networks, to plan crimes. The web makes it easier to communicate and to do business and plan with friends and family. Apparently, criminals feel that it should make planning their crimes easier, as well.

The Internet actually makes it easier for the law to catch the criminals though. First, law enforcement is able to trace the crime back to them. Even those who try to hide their tracks will soon find the law knocking on, or knocking down, their door. The online activities also become evidence the legal system will use against them when they go to court. Computer forensics specialists today can find nearly anything on electronic devices.

Committing crimes is stupid to begin with, but planning them or recording them online takes people to an entirely new level of stupid. Yet, the law apprehends individuals, and even businesses, on a nearly daily basis based on their online activities.

Confessing to Crimes... Even False Confessions is Not Bright

Chances are you've done something illegal at some point in life, although it was probably something minor. Everyone makes the occasional bad decision, and sometimes breaks the law... sometimes without really knowing it.

Even though you might feel the legal indiscretion was relatively minor, that's no reason to post about it or brag about it online. In fact, it could bring legal trouble your way before you know it. It would make sense to keep those types of indiscretions quiet, but people's brains just don't seem to work that way.

Everyone wants to have something to say. They hope that it's interesting, too, so they might talk about how they are cheating on their taxes or how they are growing their own marijuana plants. Yes, people really are that oblivious to the fact that law enforcement is actually monitoring social networks and public blogs for just this type of information. These brain surgeons are actually doing the work of law enforcement for them, complete with compiling nice lists of evidence for the courts!

It's very simple to avoid this problem. First, don't break the law. That's all there really should be to it. However, if you have broken the law, don't talk about it, especially online where anyone can see the information. Invoke an altered rule of fight club. You know... don't talk about fight club.

Web Retaliation

Internet revenge is unfortunately growing, and many people are getting sucked into the promise of sweet and anonymous vengeance. The Internet makes it easy to strike at people you know, and it is alarmingly easy to ruin someone else's life. People commit hacking crimes, cyberstalking, and more.

Some people even try to spread rumors about others through their social network. Exes do this when they feel spurned in a relationship for example. They may say horrible things about their former boyfriend or girlfriend, such as that they have an STD or that they are a bed wetter. They look for ways to humiliate the other party in some way.

Catfishing

Catfishing is another method of retaliation that is increasing in frequency online and deserved its own section here. There is even a documentary and a subsequent television show about the subject.

With this method, one person pretends to be someone else in order to get information or an action of some sort from a second party. For example, if someone were angry with a former friend, he or she could create an online alternate personality of the opposite sex and try to damage the person's relationship with his or her spouse. Some pretend to be employers looking to hire someone, someone looking for love, and more.

Old Games, More Pain

Pretending to be someone else on the web is nothing new, and people should know better than to trust someone they don't really know and that they are unable to meet in person. However, so many people fall for the con that it *continues* to happen.

It is a terrible thing to do to someone, but again, the lack of empathy the Internet seems to breed takes hold here. People don't really understand just how much damage they can cause.

Never engage in this type of activity. Even if the other people never find out what you've done, it is something you will know and have to live with. Toying with the emotions of other people is mean-spirited at best and dangerous at worst.

There really are instances of people who have been harassed and duped with online relationships that have gone on to commit suicide. Think about other people before you do something so mean spirited as pretending to be someone else to get them to open up to you only to destroy them later.

Move On and Don't Think About Revenge

Even if someone else has upset or angered you, it really is best to let it go, or at least try to let it go and to get your revenge simply by living a good and happy life instead. "Getting back" at someone through the web causes more problems, and sometimes, it can even pose legal problems.

When you try to commit online vengeance, it will come back and blow up in your face just as easily as if you were to start bragging about a crime.

Where do all of these problems occur online?
Actually, getting into trouble on the web – all types of
trouble – can happen nearly anywhere.

Social Networks

Most people in the modern world have at least one
social network account today. What social networks
are you using right now? The most popular include:

- Facebook
- Twitter
- Instagram
- Pinterest
- LinkedIn
- Google Plus
- Tumblr

These are certainly not the only social networking
sites out there, but they are the most popular, and
that means they are most likely going to be the ones

where you and others will have the highest likelihood of saying or posting something that you should not.

Posting on these sites is extraordinarily fast and easy. You can do it when you are sitting at work and are on the computer, when you are home with the laptop, or even while you are going through the apps on your smart phone. No matter where you are and what you are doing, you can post.

This presents a problem for a couple of reasons.

If you are out with your friends and having a great time, you might not think about the things you are posting. Everything is in the moment. However, other people may not see the humor, or they could be outright offended. If you have been drinking, and you are in a nice and innocent little town such as Las Vegas, then you really might not think about what you are posting.

When you put up pictures and posts for the world to see, they have an impact. People read them, see them, and then react to them. That's the way social networking works, but it constantly seems to surprise people when they start to get grief for the silly or downright stupid things they've posted without thinking.

Time Stamps

Something else you will want to remember with these social networks is that they have time stamps and date stamps on them. This will affect your personal relationships, as well as your work relationships, as you will see in the next chapter.

Let's say you and your friends want to head out for a few drinks and perhaps to visit a club. You get a call from your significant other who wants to come over, but you claim you are going to head to bed. Two hours later, they see that you are drinking and having a great time out at the club. What will they think?

They will see just how unimportant they are that you didn't bother to tell them the truth.

While you might not have intended it that way, that's how many people will actually take it. This can damage your relationship, and if you do it often enough, you could get the label of a liar.

This doesn't just have to happen with significant others either. If you tell family and friends you have to do something for work when you don't want to visit, and they see that you've gone somewhere else, they will probably not be happy.

Saying the Wrong Thing

It also happens to be quite easy to post and write the wrong thing whether you are on your page or posting a comment to something someone else said. When you start to post about some of those touchy subjects mentioned earlier, things can get dicey rather quickly.

To have the best and safest time with the social networks, it is always a good practice to make sure that you are not writing inflammatory posts. Having strong opinions can be good, but you need to make sure you know just when you should keep them to yourself.

Blogs and Sites

If you have a blog that other people can read and you call it a personal blog, then you might be deluding yourself a bit. It's personal only in the sense that it's about you, but it's not private. There is a huge difference. Some people use their blogs as though they are personal diaries, wanting to share everything with their readers.

Being open can be good, but you don't want to share too much. You also need to think about the types of posts you write. While it might be okay to bring up some controversial topics sometimes, you need to be ready for the backlash that could come from it. You also should be careful about the wording you use in your posts and any replies to comments from readers. Keep things as civil as possible so your blog doesn't suddenly become famous for a flame war that would rival the Chicago Fire.

This is important when you have your own personal blog, and it is just as important – more important some might say – when you have a blog or a website for your company. Later in the book, we'll cover how your actions online can affect the success of your business.

Forums, Sites and Online Communities

You may have quite a few sites that you visit and read regularly. Perhaps you have a couple of favorite news sites, recipe or game sites, and more. You may have some forums and other online communities that you enjoy as well. They can be quite fun and informative. Many people have just as much fun reading the comments as they do reading an actual article or the original post.

However, these communities tend to become rather negative places once the trolls take hold. The comments can become a minefield in no time, and there is always the temptation to get involved in a battle with the trolls.

You have to remember that you will never actually win one of these battles though. Yes, you might be right, and you might have good points, but they will eventually try to make you look like a fool. If you aren't careful with your words, it could work. On these sites, and any site for that matter, completely ignoring them really is the best possible option you can hope to take.

YouTube

Do you have a YouTube channel, or do you simply like watching and commenting on videos? Again, you have to be very careful. If you have a channel and you are posting content, make sure that the content is something that you really want to associate with you and your personal or professional brand.

Your Videos

Think about how others will view the content and what they will think of you when they view it. Sometimes, people put up videos of their children or their pets in conditions that some perceive as harmful. This draws anger from the Internet quickly, as you would expect.

Never post anything that could be construed as illegal either. Use your common sense when you are making videos, and if you don't have enough common sense not to perform and record illegal activities, well, then perhaps you deserve to have the law catch up to you.

Something else you will want to consider when you are posting videos is that you will be getting comments on them unless you choose to disable the comments. Many of the comments will probably be encouraging. However, others will be negative, angry, and downright nasty at times.

Remember that these are just the trolls trying to get you to come out and play. Don't fall for their traps. Simply ignore them.

Others' Videos

When you are watching videos online, you might come across some videos that irk you or that make you want to comment negatively. While you have the right to your opinion, and you certainly have the right to post, you have to use your head when you do it.

Do not post to their video as soon as you finish watching it. This applies to when you are reading posts and forum comments as well. Take some time to cool off before you write anything at all. Make your post articulate and well thought out, and never resort to name-calling. Try to have a serious dialogue.

Even if the original poster does not appreciate this and he or she resorts to dirty tactics, everyone else who sees your interactions will see you as a class act. It's always the best way to approach these situations.

Chapter 4: Damaging Your Personal Relationships

The things you do online can, and will, affect your relationships in the real world. They can damage your relationships in more ways than you might think, often because of things you post without really thinking.

Let's look at some of the things that you might post that could cause some serious issues.

Infidelity

Social networking sites, Facebook in particular, is starting to get quite a reputation as being trouble when it comes to relationships in terms of infidelity. People find that it is easy to connect with others through the platform. They could connect with strangers, people they barely know, or old friends. This is one of the great things about the social network. It lets you make some great new connections and to renew some old connections.

However, this can also breed quite a bit of trouble. It also has the ability to kindle online romances. This causes problems for many couples, and research shows that a large number of people on Facebook are unfaithful because of connections they've made through the site.

It's important to remember that Facebook, or any social network for that matter, does not cause cheating. The fault always lies with the participants, and to deny that is simply to deflect the blame from where it really should go. People were cheating on one another long before there was such a thing as Facebook. Social networks are simply platforms that make it easier to cheat.

Lack of a True Connection

It's important to mention something else that can cause some issues within relationships when it comes to social networks in particular. Many people today communicate with one another solely through their social networks, as well as their digital devices.

Instead of picking up a phone and actually *calling* the other person, they will instead write a message or a Tweet, or perhaps send a text message if they are feeling particularly full of energy. The point is that they minimize the amount of effort they are putting into the relationship. They are having less face-to-face contact and less real contact. Everything comes from the digital messages they get, and that becomes unhealthy.

When you write the wrong thing, such as a joke that doesn't land, it becomes a big deal. When you don't post enough to your page to let the other person know what's happening in your life, it can become an issue as well. When you do not have a real connection with the other person – and we're not talking about an Internet connection – it can make communication difficult.

People really need to start putting those phones and devices away so they can actually reconnect with one another.

That Funny Story

Do you remember that hilarious story you and your friends had from a couple of years ago? The one where you went to Sin City, got drunk, fell into the fountain at Caesar's Palace, and argued with a security guard about where to find some French bread.

While this might not be your exact story, you probably have your own weird and fun stories, and you might even be still making some fun stories on occasion. That doesn't mean that everyone in your personal life needs to know about it.

Your parents and grandparents who connect with you on Facebook and Google Plus might not want to know about some of the raucous times you've had. You're current girlfriend or boyfriend might not want to know about some of your fun times with exes either. It's fine that you have those great experiences and that you recall them fondly. However, you do not want to make others feel uncomfortable by rehashing a story that happened a long time ago in one of your posts.

Once more, think about how other people will view it and what they will think. Put yourself in their position.

Even YOU Can't Believe You Said That

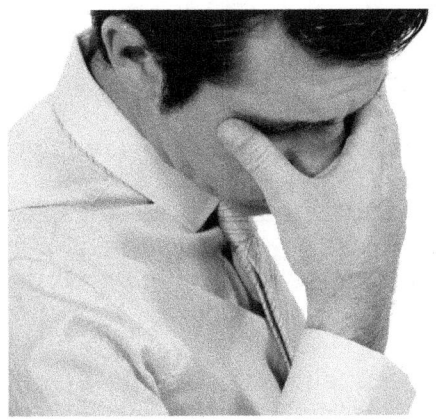

Earlier, we talked about anger and emotion as well as how it can make you say and write some stupid things sometimes. You aren't a troll and you are not a mean person. Sometimes, you can say the wrong thing though, and you can type it out and press send without thinking about the affect it will have.

It happens sometimes. We've gone over this. However, we haven't really touched on just how much damage it can do to your relationships with the people who are important to you.

A few hours, or even just a few minutes later, you start to realize the implications of what you've written. Maybe you said something misogynistic that you thought would come off as a joke. Maybe you used a bit of sarcasm and actually ended up insulting someone. The things you post can have repercussions.

You still want to be yourself, and you don't want to hammer that censor button any more than you need to, but thinking about how others will view it can help you from posting things that you will regret.

Think twice, post once. Or, don't post at all, if you feel that it could cause trouble in your private life. Ultimately, you are the only one who will be able to determine what your circle of family and friends will and will not accept without feeling hurt.

Too Sensitive?

Self-censorship can be a good thing and a bad thing. When you use your brain to keep from posting things that are truly harmful to your personal relationships, it is certainly helpful. However, just as you've noticed that the world today seems a bit crueler than usual because of the perceived disconnect the web can provide, you have to admit that the world has become far more sensitive at the same time. Some might say that the world is overly sensitive to every little thing, and they might be right.

No matter what you post, there is a chance that it will offend someone or will get him or her to respond negatively to you.

For example, you could post about having a great day and loving being able to get out into the sunshine. Someone could reply saying that the area is in a drought and the sunny weather is actually not a good thing. They'll harp about the drought and fire season and make your good day feel somehow shameful. In this case, they are in the wrong, but you might feel wrong for having posted at all.

Censor yourself if you think you are saying something that might be actually offensive or in bad taste, but don't get to the point where you are afraid to post *anything* because you worry about how people are going to take it. Just use common sense when you post and everything will be fine.

Really.

Meeting Someone Special

You've had plenty of fun in your time, and like many people, you've catalogued a good chunk of that fun online. While it's nice to have some photos of your vacation, your family and friends, and whatnot on the social networks for people to see, you might want to rethink some of the types of information you put up there.

When you finally meet someone, a new love interest in your life, and you are going on your first few dates, do you know what one of the first things he or she is likely to do? Chances are good the person will check out your online activity.

Keep in mind that this is not spying if you have your information out there publicly and on display for the world to see. People today look up others online as a means of defense, so they can learn a bit more about the person they are dating and know whether they are A.) Safe to Date and B.) The Right Match.

At first, people tend to look for the Big Things – evidence of arrest and the like. However, if you have profiles displayed publicly or if you connect with the person online so he or she has access to see your posts and photos, you can bet they will look. It's part curiosity and part self-preservation on their part. They want to know more about you before they invest time in you.

So, you really need to be careful of what you post. You might be a great guy or gal, but some of your posts might make you come off a bit... less than worthy. Photos of you waltzing into a strip club, drinking until even your photos are blurry, or posts that start with, "Oh, my God! I was so drunk last night..." will not paint you in the best light in the eyes of someone looking to date you. In fact, these types of posts probably won't look great in the eyes of a potential employer either, but we'll get to that later.

This does not mean you should ever lie or keep anything important from someone who might become a significant other in your life, but it does mean you should seriously consider some of the benefits that discretion is capable of offering.

Where Are You Now?

Here is another way that the things you post on the Internet can come back to cause harm. This one is something countless people do all the time without ever thinking about the implications.

Vacation Time

You are a hard worker, and you deserve to take some much-needed time away from the workplace. After putting in 40, 50, or even 60 hours a week, everyone needs to have a nice little getaway. While you are at it, why not let everyone in your social network and everyone who reads your blog know that you are heading out on vacation too! After all, wouldn't they be happy to know you are finally getting some time away?

Although you might feel as if you can trust your close family and friends implicitly, you never know who else might find out you will be away on vacation. Never put up the dates you will be going out of town, as this simply becomes an open invitation to thieves and would-be burglars to make their way into your home.

Yet, people are always putting up their every move online, even though common sense dictates that it's a terrible idea. They post about everything that they do and where they are. When you read most people's feeds, you will see when they are going on vacation and when they will be away. Some people even post their full itinerary on their social networks.

This is highly dangerous, as most people should realize. You don't need to let everyone know where you are.

Remember that the items you post are time stamped, as we mentioned earlier in the chapter. This means if you start posting your great beach photos from Maui to your account, then everyone who can view it will know that you aren't in your Chicago home. Again, most of the time, this is not a problem since you can trust family and friends. However, do you really want to take that chance?

Have only a select number of people in your inner circle know when you are on vacation and wait until you get home to post all of your great stories and photos. If you do plan to post photos on the go, as so many people want to do, then the very least you should do is have someone watch over your home while you are away.

Personal Safety

While we are on the subject, it is a good idea to think about the things you post online and your personal safety, as well as the safety of your family members.

So many people really seem ignorant of the dangers in the world, as well as just how easy it is to find out information about a person through social networks.

Putting up information about where you will be or having your social networks "check in" for you when you arrive at different places can be a very bad idea. Letting everyone know that you are at Disney World or that you are enjoying a meal at your favorite restaurant might seem like an innocent enough post – and it should be – but you have to be wary of who will see the message.

For example, if you don't want all of your family and friends to know where you are, and what you are doing every minute of the day, then don't keep checking in everywhere you go.

Also, consider that some people you don't want to see might find out where you are and show up uninvited. This has happened to people who check in on a social network and all of a sudden, a jealous or angry ex shows up at the exact same spot.

If you, or anyone you know, has ever had to deal with a stalker, then you should be extra cautious about putting this sort of information up online.

Along the same lines, consider the information you post about your children. You don't need people to know when and where their sports practices are or where their school is. You do not need to let people you don't know, or barely know, in on anything about your children or family for that matter.

Consider the pictures that you are putting up online and really look at them before you post. Do any of them that are in or outside of your home show the street address or any identifying features that could clue someone in as to where you live?

Putting out all of this type of information can be a very bad idea, since you do not want the wrong people getting it. People really didn't have to worry about this before the trend of social networking and putting every little move we make on the web. People today make it far too easy for those who wish to do them harm.

Does all of this sound a bit paranoid? Well, it might be, at least a little. However, is there really any such thing as too safe when it comes to your family and to your own personal safety?

Think About These Family Posts

Whenever you are thinking about putting up a post, whether it is a Little League schedule, photos of the family, or a mid-vacation brag post, think about the people who will see it and who could see it. Do you really want all of them to have that information? Instead of blasting it out to the entire world, use email, or send it only to specific people in your friends and connections list on Facebook and other social sites.

This still lets you put up the information you want about your vacation, your family, and anything else that you like. However, it limits the number of people who can post it. Whenever you have the option, consider putting your settings to private so you can limit access.

Sexting and Private Home Videos

There's nothing wrong with having a healthy sex life, and there's nothing wrong with making your own private videos or sending intimate text messages to the person that you love. However, you have to be careful what happens with these texts and videos. Imagine what would happen if you accidently sent them to the wrong people?

It could be disastrous, and this sort of thing happens far more than you might imagine. In fact, there's even a movie with Jason Segel and Cameron Diaz, which covers this exact subject. The movie is a comedy, but if this happens to you, you can bet it is going to be more horror than laughs.

Who Else Loves When You Share Too Much?

We know that thieves and stalkers are over the moon about people sharing too much on Facebook and other social networks. Do you know who else loves it? Lawyers, as it can help them in cases against or for or you and it can actually provide evidence. It has the potential to be a double-edged sword.

If you are a great person and only post great things on Facebook, then an attorney can use it to establish your character, and even use those time stamped posts to show that you have an alibi for a crime.

However, if you post some unflattering things on the site, such as photos of you doing illicit drugs, drinking to excess, and more, it can harm you. If you are posting angry rants, racial jokes, or misogynistic comments, it will most certainly work against you – when it comes to building a character profile and in life in general. The lawyers can use this information to establish just what type of person you really are.

Think about how this could work against someone. If you are in a custody battle, for example, and you have any of the aforementioned types of posts, whom do you think the court will side with in this case? You or the other parent?

The answer should be obvious.

With negativity all over your online footprint, you will not be winning the hearts and minds of the judge or jury.

If you post something when upset or under the influence and then delete it a few hours, or even just a few minutes later, the damage could still be done. Someone may have taken a screenshot of the post.

If you send an email, you can't take it back. Once it is out in the wild, it's out there for good and you have to live with the consequences of it.

It's Not Rocket Science

Even though the Internet's been around for some time now, we're really still in the Wild West stages of the web. With all of the new types of tech and gadgets, and social networks that people can become a part of, we're bringing technology into our personal lives at a faster rate than ever before.

Many people are adapting well, but others simply don't get the basics of online etiquette. By adhering to the same etiquette that you would extend in the real world, you will find that you should get along quite well online.

If you are generally calm in the real world and you wouldn't jump up and start calling someone names or tell an off color joke, then you should not have much trouble succeeding on the Internet without getting into much trouble at all.

Of course, if you are quick to anger in real life and you don't always think before speaking, you probably won't think before posting. Trouble will come your way unless you are willing to change your ways.

It's not rocket science.

Simply use your head and good judgment before you put anything up online.

Chapter 5: Problems at the Workplace

We've looked at the ways that your posts and pictures can affect your personal life, and now it's time to see how your actions on the Internet can affect your job. In fact, the things you post online could end up getting you fired if you are not careful.

If you post about the company, whether it is good or bad, there could be repercussions based on the business's policies. Most companies today realize that people are online and using social media, blogging, and posting photos and videos all the time, so they've added elements into their employee guides through human resources to address these things.

Let's look at some of the ways you can get in trouble posting on the web about, or at, your workplace.

Violation of Company Policy

All companies are different, and it is important for you to know your company's particular policies. Some have rather obtuse and hard to understand rules, which give the company leeway when it comes to firing you, so make sure you not only know the regulations, but that you actually understand what they mean, as well.

Some companies will allow you to post about the company, but you are limited as to the types of things you can say. For example, they do not want you badmouthing your boss or the company in general.

Even though you might have some negative feelings about the place or your boss, you need to keep them to yourself rather than putting them out on the social networks for everyone to see. It is bad form, and it will not endear you to anyone at the company that might have been able to help you if you were really having issues.

They Will Know... They Always Know

If you think they will never see your Facebook post or Tweet, you are sorely mistaken. Most companies today, at least the smart ones, track their mentions online. Whenever the name of the company, and perhaps even the management, is posted they have alerts so they can see the post or Tweet. Your Tweets go right into Google, so it is only a matter of time – a very short amount of time – before the company finds it. When they do, you can imagine they will not be very happy.

You also have to think about your coworkers who are also your friends on these social networks. They may not like what you have to say about the company. They might even have ambitions to get a higher position, and alerting the bosses to your posts might just be something they would do in order to be in favor of the influential people at the company.

If you are using a company computer, keep in mind that some businesses will track where you go and what you do when you are online. After all, you are using their equipment and their resources. They may restrict access to some parts of the web, and they may monitor others.

In fact, some companies will also monitor email exchanges between employees that happen on their intranet within the company. Since everything should be work related and they let employees know up front, they can do this legally.

Whether someone does it deliberately or has a "slip of the fingers" without realizing they were posting a secret, all sorts of private information has leaked online because of employees and their love of being on the web.

Your company likely has policies against this. Most have nondisclosure agreements for sensitive information, and this certainly extends to social media, blogs, and the like, as well as verbal communication. When they say you can't speak about something, they also mean that you can't write about something. There is no wiggle room in this.

Yet, we constantly hear about leaks from movie sets, videogame and tech companies, and much more. Sometimes, the leaks are actually intentional. Other times, they are employees who posted without thinking, or who posted because they were trying to get back at the company for some reason.

A good rule of thumb is simply to not post anything about your company online. That way, you never have to wonder if what you said was a secret that you should not divulge or not.

Looking for Work... at Work

Here is yet another bad idea that people continue to do. They are unhappy with their job, so they decide to spend a good chunk of their time looking for a new career. That's generally a good idea. If you are unhappy somewhere, it's time to start looking for a better place to be, so you can be happy.

However, looking for that other place during the day while you are at your current job and supposed to be working is *not* such a great idea. Do not use the company resources and time to be looking for another job.

Do that on your own time, or else you might find that you get your wish – not having to come to work – sooner than you thought. The only downside is that you will not be getting a paycheck either. Just look for work on your own time like the rest of the world has to do.

In fact, you'll find that spending time online doing anything not directly related to your job is going to cause problems. Many companies today are complaining that their employees are increasingly spending their time staring at and playing with their phones or using their work computers to access the web for personal reasons.

If you want to keep on the good side of the management at work, you'll save your Internet activities for breaks, lunch, and off work.

Unflattering Personal Posts

The things you say and post online that don't directly have anything to do with the company could actually cause some trouble in the workplace, as well. Even when you aren't at work, you could be representing the company, particularly if people actually know whom you work for when you post. With Facebook, for example, people can see your workplace.

People who post slurs, who troll online and start trouble, or who post photos of themselves taking drugs could have others report them to their company. Those companies do not want to associate with people who could possibly show the company in a negative light.

Most states have at-will employment. This means you can quit your job whenever you want for whatever reasons you want. In fact, you don't even need to have a reason. However, this goes both ways. In addition to being able to quit when you like, the company has the right to fire you whenever they want without giving a reason. Most will provide grounds, but they do not need to.

If you are making the company somehow look bad online because of your behavior, chances are very good they will fire you. They may give you a warning, but they do not have to.

While this might not seem fair and it might seem like an invasion of privacy because people are posting in their personal life, it does make sense. You would not want to associate with someone who made you continually look bad. Your company is the same way, and they are in business *to make money*. They can't let you do anything that might tarnish their brand.

Blogging, Social Networking and Your Job Search

What if you don't have a job yet and are just now starting the hunt? How could your online activities affect it? You will see that it can have much the same effect for the same types of reasons.

Are you a blogger? Many people today blog, or have a Tumblr account, which is almost a pseudo blog. Others have the equivalent of blog posts on Facebook.

Even if you have just a small blog with a few readers, it is important to be careful of what you post on there. Your prospective employers will look up your name when you send in a resume or put in an application. They do this so they can look at your online footprint.

An online or digital footprint is the term used for the digital tracks that people leave on the web. This includes a variety of different things, including some that employers will easily be able to find. Here are just some of the elements that make up your online history.

- Online registrations
- Social network posts
- Uploaded photos
- Uploaded videos
- Emails and attachments
- Blog posts

If you've ever done any of these things, then you have a footprint online. The things you've done add up to your online reputation, and the things that you write in your blogs are online for everyone to see. You can be sure when an employer does a search of your name that blogs, and much of this other information, such as the posts, photos, and videos, will come up.

Take a moment to think about how you would fare if someone looked up your name. In fact, don't just think about it. Instead, go to Google or your favorite search engine right now and type in your name, and variants of your name, so you can see what the employers will find.

What did you find? Was it better or worse than you thought? It's time that you did something about it.

If you have issues with your online reputation right now and you feel that you might not be able to get a job, don't worry quite yet. You don't have to throw in the towel, as there is some help out there for you.

Are You Friends With the Boss?

Your boss might want to connect with you on Facebook and other sites. It can be a good idea to accept the request if you absolutely love your job and there is no chance of ever putting anything unflattering – about you or the company – online. However, you really do need to think twice about this. It can be good… or bad. Forget about taking a "sick" day off from work to go fishing, or at least forget about posting about it on your page.

Getting Help

You will want to limit the amount of negative content online if you can. In Chapter 7, we'll discuss how you can do this in detail. It's not always easy, but it is possible to do on your own.

If you find that it is simply too much to handle on your own though, there are actually specialists out there who can help to brighten your online reputation for a fee. In some cases, they are well worth the cost.

When choosing someone to help you with your online reputation, check into the experience the company has in the field. It's relatively new, but you want to know that they've been in business for more than a week, and you want to know the types of things they will do to help improve your reputation on the web.

Some Parting Tips to Smart Posting

Here are just a few quick tips you can use to make sure you are posting smart so that you don't have any troubles at work.

- Keep posts about work confidential.
- If in doubt, don't post.
- Never send a resume from your current job.
- Always post smart.
- Be ready for the repercussions.
- If posting something seems like it could be a bad idea, don't do it.

Chapter 6: Destroying Your Business and Your Brand

Perhaps you don't work for anyone else. Maybe you are your own boss with your own business. You might be a solo entrepreneur, or you could own a small but growing business. Maybe you are the owner of a large company that wants to keep on getting bigger and stronger.

Since you are technically the boss, should you be able to post whatever you want online without repercussions? While you probably won't fire yourself, there will still be backlash from thoughtless, mean spirited, or just plain ridiculous posts.

Easy Ways to Destroy Your Business Online

News spreads quickly on the web, and when you post something that you shouldn't it spreads even faster. Damaging your brand with thoughtless posts is far easier than you might imagine, and it can take time and a substantial amount of effort to win back the people who may no longer feel as though they like or can even trust your company.

Companies do things that damage their brand with their online posts all the time, and their posting sins generally fall into one of several very specific categories.

Playing Off the News

It's good to stay current with the times and the latest trends. However, it is not a good idea to turn current event stories into marketing ploys, especially those that have potential emotional reactions to them. Most of the time, this will backfire on you because people feel that it is in bad taste, and they see that it is merely a marketing attempt.

They tend not to like it, and it is even worse when companies make jokes about something that is a tragedy.

At best, they will ignore it. However, if the subject you try to use for marketing is a touchy one, people will pile onto your company with a load of negativity.

Social media can work wonders for marketing and publicity for you, but as soon as there is a bit of blood in the water, the Twitter sharks and others will attack, so you have to be careful.

Inappropriate Posts and Images

You want to use your social networks and blogs as a way to build a better relationship with customers, but you do not want to get to the point where you are putting up images and posts that are too familiar. They are customers, not friends and family that would better understand your sense of humor.

Some companies have actually been in trouble for sending nude and semi-nude photos to their customers. You are in control of what you post, and if you have employees, you need to make sure that they are not posting anything untoward on behalf of your company.

If you post anything sexual, politically or religiously charged, or controversial, you can expect reactions on the web, and they will not always be in your favor.

Know Your Brand and the Types of Messages You Can Use

Different brands have different niches and different customers. Some will be able to get away with certain types of posts while others will not. Comedians, for example, tend to have more leeway when it comes to posting jokes and off color humor on their site and social networks. A bank president would not have that same amount of leeway with his or her posts.

Different professions are treated differently when it comes to what they can post, so you really do need to know your role and your niche.

Know Your Connections

Whom do you work with regularly? How much do you know about those people or other companies? What if you found out that one of your suppliers once used, or is still using, child labor in China? What would happen when your customers find this out? What would happen if you worked with someone who has a record for fraud, or just about any other crime for that matter? This has the potential to damage your business when people find out, as well.

You need to be aware of everyone you work with in every capacity possible, and you have to put in the due diligence to research those people as much as you can. Just as you searched for your own online reputation with Google, you can do the same thing with those other companies and people.

A little research on these people and companies, and your employees, can save you quite a bit of grief later.

Be Ready

You are responsible for the things you post, and you need to be smart about it. However, if you have employees, it can sometimes be difficult to rein them in, and sometimes you *still* might post without thinking even after reading this book.

If that happens, you need to be ready for the repercussions, and you need to take action to mend the problem before it really damages your brand and your business. In Chapter 8, we'll look at some of those times when companies, as well as individuals, did not take action soon enough.

Here are some of the things that you should do to help you keep your reputation in good shape after posting something online that you shouldn't have.

Tips for Managing Your Brand Reputation

When you've made an error with your online content in some way, whether it was a thoughtless post or anything else that threatens to damage the company's online, and possibly offline, reputation, keep the following in mind.

Be Honest

First, you need to make sure that you do not try to hide the fact that you or someone in the company did something wrong. When you are honest and work to get to the bottom of the issue, you will have more control of the story and how it unfolds. Even though people may not like the photo or post, being honest about what happened should at least earn more respect from detractors.

If you try to hide it, it will eventually come out, and then your company will look even worse. Control the situation. Do not let it control you.

Apologize

If you or the company has done something wrong, then you need to own up to it, as mentioned, but you also need to issue a sincere apology. Hardly a week goes by without someone from a prominent company, a celebrity, or some other high profile individual comes out to make an apology for something they've done.

Often, they have to apologize for indiscretions that appeared online.

When apologizing, you need to be sincere about it. The damage is done, but the apology can help to minimize it if people feel it is genuine.

Remove the Problem

What happened? Where did things fail? Find out what occurred and who made the post or sent the text that started the uproar and make sure that person receives appropriate punishment. Often, this means terminating the person's employment. If you were at fault, think long and hard about what you did and make sure that it is not something that you repeat.

Regain Control

Once you take care of the damage, it's time to regain control of the business and make sure you have a plan in place to ensure this sort of thing does not happen again. Start putting out as much positive press as you can to help reduce the negative effects the mishap caused.

Chapter 7: Wrecking and Repairing Your Reputation

So far, we've looked at all of the different ways that people can ruin their reputation online. We've seen how it can affect their personal relationships and how some posts can even lead to dangerous situations. We've looked at how it can damage your work, and even your brand if you own your own business.

Hopefully, you've discovered that it's possible to mitigate many of these problems simply by *thinking before you post*. A little thought really can go a long way.

OPP

Let's check out one other thing that can really damage your reputation without it even really being your fault. If you've been diligent about being wary about the things you post, there is still a chance that there could be some things out there about you that you don't want people to see. Namely… OPP – other people's pictures.

If someone has some funny, embarrassing, or racy photos of you and they decide to post them online along with your name, such as on Facebook, then those pictures will show op when people search for your name.

Un-tag your name from those pictures on Facebook, and simply let the person who posted it know why you did so. If the photos are not on Facebook and are on another site, requires that the person who posted them remove your name, just to make them more difficult to find.

This will help your personal relationships, as well as your work life and your own personal brand. Don't overlook the things other people post!

You Wrecked It... Now Fix It

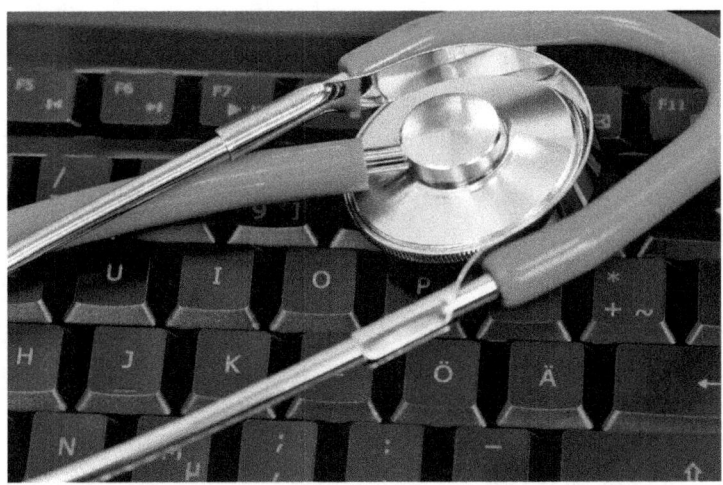

However, you might be at a point where it's a little bit too late. You've already wrecked your reputation, or at least put a heck of a dent in it and now you don't know what to do. Maybe you don't have the money to hire someone to repair the damage for you. Many people don't.

If that's the case, you can do some things that will help, and it's actually quite easy to do. You simply have to be willing to put in the time and the effort to do it.

Let's get into the things you need to do so you can get started.

Search Your Name(s)

We've already mentioned the very first thing you should do in an earlier chapter. Search for yourself on Google and other search engines to see what comes up in the results. The items on the first two or three pages are what people will see when they look up your name or your business's name.

What shows up? Is it good or bad? If it's good, then throw up your feet and relax for a bit because you don't have anything else to do. If it's bad, or even just a *little* bad, get ready to do a bit of work.

Check Privacy Settings on Social Networks

One of the most important things you will want to do is make sure that you check the privacy settings on all of your social networks and online accounts. You want to make sure everything is private if you don't want everyone and his brother to be able to find out more about you. You can do this on Facebook, as well as on sites such as YouTube.

Always look into the privacy settings and make the outlet as private as you need. Of course, if you are running a business, you can't keep everything private. For individuals though, it's a good idea to keep things private so you have more control over the information that's out there "in the wild" about you.

Look at Your Blog

Read your blog, even the old posts, and look for items that might be a bit unflattering or that are controversial and think about how much you really need those posts. Blogs show up in the search engines, and if you are using your blog to vent your anger and frustrations about this or that, it could result in trouble.

You don't have to censor your views or passion necessarily, but you should probably revisit the blog and consider checking the language and editing to make sure it comes off less like a crazy, profane rant.

Think about what others might say or think when they view it and remove anything that would come across as unprofessional.

Use Your Head

Your head is for more than looking beautiful or handsome and holding your favorite hats. We have said it before, and really, we can't say it enough. You need to think before you post *anything* online today.

People are always watching and they are always looking for a reason to pounce on you. They'll even pounce on the posts that are innocuous, so you do not want to give them any real reasons to be upset!

Dealing with Embarrassing Content About You Already Online

What if there is already a bunch of items about you online already, and what if it is less than flattering? As mentioned, you can hire someone to help you take care of your online reputation. However, you can do some things on your own as well.

First, contact the person who put up the embarrassing information, such as a picture of you on Facebook, and ask if they would remove it. Chances are it is someone you know who put up the photo, and as long as you are on good terms with the person, it should be easy enough to have them remove it for you.

If they aren't agreeable to taking it off, and you feel as though you are at your wit's end, consider contacting the site, or site host, about the content. For example, if someone, such as an ex, refuses to take down certain photos on the site, get in touch with Facebook directly. They don't make this easy, but you have a few different ways of contacting them and getting some action.

The following tips are purposely generic, so they will apply to *most* of the different social networks and sites.

- Post in their help forums.
- Submit a complaint for violating terms or for intellectual property infringement, depending

on the nature of the material you want
removed.

- Send an email to their support site.
- Call them.

Make the Content Disappear

Another good way to make some of the embarrassing
content about you go away is by burying it in the
search results. Most people don't look past the first
couple of pages on Google, which is why so many
people and companies struggle to maintain a high
ranking in the search engine results pages.

This actually makes it easier for you to push that
negative content deeper into the results pages. Just
start creating more of your own content and accounts.
Create a YouTube channel, accounts on photo sites,
start an account on Blogger, consider buying your
name as a domain name, and more.

When you start posting content to those sites under your own name, it begins to take up the top spots on those search results pages. When people start to search for your name, whether they are friends and family, customers or people who will potentially employ you, they will only see the good results.

Once you set everything up, you have to manage it properly. This simply means that you will want to post relatively often, and that you will want to make sure you aren't posting things that could come back to haunt you.

We've gone over the type of things that you don't want to post earlier in the book, but, essentially, if you have any doubt about whether you should post something or not, then *don't post that*!

Chapter 8: Back to Bite You

Now it's time to sit back and have a little bit of voyeuristic fun at the misfortunes of others. Of course, we're not really reveling in the mistakes that other people and companies have made on the web. Rather, it's important to look at the different ways that others have caused trouble on the web so you can see how you can avoid those and similar problems.

Politicians

It's always interesting to see just how much trouble politicians can get into online. They are elected officials that we hope will lead us into better times, and they seem to have more trouble understanding how the web really works than most people. This results in some spectacular problems. Once you see some of the things they've done, you'll see it is amazing these people are elected for *anything* at all.

Let's look at some of the most prominent problems politicians have faced on the Internet.

Bob Carleton

Bob Carleton, a councilman from Norwalk, OH, sent out an email with a racist story in it that he thought was humorous. The 71-year-old, who did not create the story and simply forwarded it, did not see anything wrong with the story, even though it was blatantly racist.

In fact, he was so sure of his actions, he did not even bother to apologize for doing it. If he had, you could be sure it would not have been sincere.

Ted Cruz

Recently, marijuana was legalized in Colorado, even though it is still against federal law. Ted Cruz, Texas senator, said that because it was still illegal federally, that they should round up and arrest the pot smokers. This is coming from Ted Cruz and the Tea Party group, which generally wants the federal government to stay out of state affairs... so, there does not seem to be much logic behind what he said. It did get some negative attention though.

Jack Kingston

Jack Kingston, a congressman from Georgia, wrote that poor children in the state who did not have enough money for lunch at school and who were getting free lunches should have to work for those lunches. While this was enough to raise the ire of some, the information that came out later showed Kingston in his true light.

You see, Kingston had expensed from the taxpayers $4,182 worth of lunches for his office in three years. No one gets a free lunch except for Kingston and his cronies, it seems!

Anthony Weiner

The unfortunately named Anthony Weiner, a now former member of the U.S. House of Representatives, is one of the repeat offenders when it comes to online stupidity and not knowing – or caring – what happens. He got in trouble when he sent racy pictures of himself, and sexting, to someone who was not his wife, and the information became public.

He apologized, tried to continue his life and career, and eventually ran for mayor of New York. At that time, a second scandal broke… for doing the same thing. This time, he was using his alias, Carlos Danger (yes, that was really his alias), and he was sending texts and photos to at least three women.

Sports Stars

They might be able to perform amazing feats on the field and the court, but many athletes tend to have met their match when it comes to the Internet and how to post on it without saying something that will ultimately get them in trouble.

Tyler Seguin

Tyler Seguin, a recent acquisition of the Dallas Stars hockey team was recently in trouble for posting homophobic Tweets – not his first time doing it. The Dallas Stars quickly put a bit of distance between themselves and Sequin, saying they did not agree with his posts.

Brett Favre

Brett Favre was once one of the most respected quarterbacks ever to step onto an NFL field. People knew him as being a "tough guy", a champion who would work hard to bring his team victory no matter how far down they might be. Then, he retired for the first time, went to other teams, retired, came back, and started to have a few more problems that became public.

The one that interests us most in the nature of this book though is the very private picture and texts he sent to Jenn Sterger.

Celebrities

For some reason, people really love celebrities. They even respect them in some cases, and put them up on a pedestal that, really, they probably don't deserve. They are people just like everyone else. The only difference is that they have a different set of skills and they chose a different career path.

Just like everyone else, they can say some stupid things on the Internet as well, and they seem to do it quite often.

Let's look at some of the things celebrities have said that have changed the way people look at them, and not in a good way.

Gwyneth Paltrow

This *Iron Man* and *The Avengers* actress might be a good Pepper Potts in those films, but she doesn't always think about the words she posts to her blog and other online outlets, or in interviews. This book has been about Internet comments and trolls. Yes, they are a pain, and they can be psychologically damaging.

However, she equated mean comments on the Internet to being the same as war. There is a big difference between reading an angry comment and having someone shoot at or try to stab you. She also said that her job as an actress was more difficult than being a mother who was trying to have a career and raise children. Most mothers who do not attend red carpet events would beg to differ.

Gilbert Gottfried

Comedian Gilbert Gottfried made jokes about the tsunami that hit Japan a couple of years ago. He had been the voice of the Aflac duck, but his jokes on Twitter made a large number of people quite angry, and the insurance company decided very quickly to fire him.

Reporters

Reporters, who use their words for a living, should really know better, but they post stupid things, as well. They should understand how their words will affect others, but they continue to make mistake after mistake.

James Taranto

A writer for the *Wall Street Journal*, James Taranto, wrote that women were to blame for the rise of fatherless children in the country. He said that economic independence that women enjoy today gives them less of a reason to get married, which he felt meant that more children would be raised without fathers.

You can imagine the storm this caused.

Tarek Khamis

Social media can get people into more trouble than merely facing some backlash over a thoughtless post. It can actually get people arrested. The Palestinian Authority arrested journalist Tarek Khamis after he wrote a comment on Facebook that merely referred to another arrest the PA made earlier.

Companies

You have to remember that companies have people behind them. People who are just as fallible as anyone else is and who can fall victim to the same bad ideas of using the wrong jokes, and of saying the wrong things.

Here are some of the biggest mistakes companies have made just in the social media realm over the past few years.

Kenneth Cole

During the 2011 protests in Egypt, a Tweet from the company mentioned the "uproar", and said that it must have been because people were excited that their new line of clothes for the spring was online. They then added a link to their store. It came across as very insensitive.

Kmart

Once you get over the shock of realizing that Kmart still exists, the Tweet they posted will shock you further. After the Newtown shootings, they posted with their condolences. This would have been fine if they had not decided to add a promotional hashtag to the end of their Tweet.

The NRA

Just a few hours after the shooting in Aurora, Colorado, the NRA sent out a tweet that started "Good morning, shooters". While they say that the person who sent out the tweet did not know about the shooting, and that it was a scheduled tweet, it still made quite a few people angry.

Tesco

This is darkly funny, or not funny at all depending on your sense of humor. The company once posted a tweet that read, "…sleepy time so we're off to hit the hay!" The problem is that when they sent this out was the same time that they were dealing with the fact that there had been horsemeat found in some of the food they were selling. As they say, hay's for horses, and this certainly did not go over well with the public.

Amy's Baking Company Boutique & Bistro

This one really takes the cake, so to speak. The company had a huge Internet meltdown that was fascinating and frightening to watch. The bakery was the subject of the television show *Kitchen Nightmares*, and Gordon Ramsay was trying to help Amy and Samy Bouzaglo's struggling business. The entire thing was a disaster.

They started responding harshly to negative comments made about them rather than ignoring them, which led to an all-out war on Facebook. The owners started writing angrier and more disjointed posts, name-calling, and more. This spilled over to Reddit and Yelp as well.

Eventually, they had to hire a PR company to help them out of the mess, but the damage was already done.

Scratching the Surface

This is just the start of all of the companies, athletes, and celebrities who have been in trouble for things they've said or done online. You could spend days just looking at all of the different things that companies have said that have landed them in hot water on the Internet.

These types of things happen on a weekly and, by now, perhaps even a daily basis. It might be funny if it weren't simultaneously so tragic that people simply don't stop to think about the things they post.

Keep your eyes open, and you are sure to see many more coming your way. Use them as a continuing lesson for things that you should not do online.

Chapter 9: Parting Tips to Keep Your Reputation and Your Relationships Intact

We're almost at the end, and we thought it would be a good idea to post a list of some condensed and simple-to-remember tips that you can take along with you. These are those simple and common sense tips the book has been trying to get across and that will keep you safe from doing things online that you shouldn't.

- Don't feed the trolls.
- Step away from the computer when you are angry or upset – never rage post!
- Never assume your posts or comments are anonymous. There is always a way to find out who you are.
- Don't let people on social networks know where you are going and when you will be on vacation or even out to dinner.

- Don't post racy photos.
- Don't tell off color jokes
- Don't look for work from your computer at your current job.
- Don't post negative things about your current job or the one for which you are applying.

Love and enjoy the Internet. Just make sure you know that the things you post on there can and do come back to haunt you. Take these tips and the information from the rest of the book, and stay safe and happy without any web snafus.

And when in doubt...*don't post that*!

Conclusion:

There you have it.

We've gazed into the dark side of the web, and all of the different types of things that people should simply *not* post on it. Most of it is common sense, but sometimes, emotions can get the better of us and we may want to post something or send out an email without thinking. Hopefully, this book has shown you some of the consequences of what can happen if you do that.

We've looked at the way it can harm your family and friends, and how it can demolish a career and stall your own business. We've seen, and maybe even chuckled at, a few of the real world examples of how people have been ruining their careers and lives with aplomb by posting on the web without thinking about the consequences.

Use It Wisely

The Internet is a tool. Like all other tools, it can be very beneficial. It can help you build a career, and build friendships and relationships that last for a long time. It can help you connect with people across the world and to reconnect with old friends from school you never imagined you would hear from again.

However, just as any tool, such as a hammer or a knife, can do good things, it can also do bad, particularly when you abuse it. When you don't think about what you are doing and writing on the web, when you let your anger and emotions get the better of you, and when you start posting without thinking it can go very wrong.

You must never let the Internet or your anger get the better of you. It is alarmingly easy to let it happen though. Whenever you feel the urge to post something or to send an email when you are upset, take a moment to step away from the computer to calm down and to organize your thoughts.

One Simple Rule to Live By

Remember the best and simplest rule you need to make sure you don't run into trouble on the Internet is just... *don't post that!*

Resources:

http://guyism.com/lifestyle/7-things-that-make-people-on-the-internet-very-angry.html

http://www.scientificamerican.com/article/why-is-everyone-on-the-internet-so-angry/

http://www.cracked.com/article_18554_5-wacky-internet-pranks-that-can-get-you-jail-time.html

http://abcnews.go.com/US/trolls-make-trouble-internet/story?id=20659477

http://www.theguardian.com/media/2013/aug/03/how-to-stop-trolls-social-media

http://www.reevesfirm.com/social-media-can-get-you-in-trouble-be-careful-what-you-tweet/

http://mashable.com/2012/11/25/social-media-business-disasters-2012/

http://www.buzzfeed.com/ariellecalderon/19-companies-that-made-huge-social-media-fails

http://www.smartplanet.com/photos/10-brands-damaged-by-social-media-disasters/

http://www.businessinsider.com/people-arrested-for-facebook-posts-2013-7?op=1

http://performancing.com/the-3-dumbest-ways-to-get-in-legal-trouble-online/

http://lifehacker.com/5850288/how-to-fix-internet-embarrassments-and-improve-your-online-reputation

http://netsecurity.about.com/od/securityadvisorie1/a/The-Dangers-Of-Facebook-Oversharing.htm

http://www.businessinsider.com/the-top-10-corporate-social-media-disasters-2013-11

http://www.informationweek.com/software/social/10-worst-social-media-meltdowns-of-2013/d/d-id/1112936

http://www.vice.com/en_uk/read/why-is-everyone-so-angry-on-the-internet

http://nakedsecurity.sophos.com/2012/05/24/internet-revenge-violence/

http://www.medicaldaily.com/too-much-social-media-overuse-can-damage-romantic-relationships-244968

http://newsone.com/2865300/facebook-cheating/

http://jobsearch.about.com/od/jobsearchblogs/a/jobsearchblog.htm

http://jobsearch.about.com/od/jobsearchprivacy/a/postingonline.htm

http://www.boston.com/jobs/galleries/workfriendlyfacebook/

http://www.forbes.com/sites/jacquelynsmith/2013/04/16/how-social-media-can-help-or-hurt-your-job-search/

http://career-advice.monster.com/in-the-office/workplace-issues/mixing-online-social-networking-with-work-hot-jobs/article.aspx

http://www.webopedia.com/TERM/D/digital_footprint.html

http://www.socialmediaexaminer.com/cleaning-your-digital-footprint/

http://www.forbes.com/sites/kevinharrington/2013/12/05/6-quick-fix-tips-for-reputation-repair/

https://smallbusiness.yahoo.com/advisor/blogs/profit-minded/how-social-media-can-ruin-your-brand-s-online-reputation-214743670.html

http://www.forbes.com/sites/susanadams/2013/03/14/6-steps-to-managing-your-online-reputation/

https://brandyourself.com/info/seo/online_reputation

http://www.salary.com/10-ways-to-improve-your-online-reputation/

http://lifehacker.com/5850288/how-to-fix-internet-embarrassments-and-improve-your-online-reputation

http://www.alternet.org/tea-party-and-right/9-right-wingers-who-said-and-did-colossally-stupid-things-week?page=0%2C2

www.ingramcontent.com/pod-product-compliance
Lightning Source LLC
Chambersburg PA
CBHW051214170526
45166CB00005B/1896